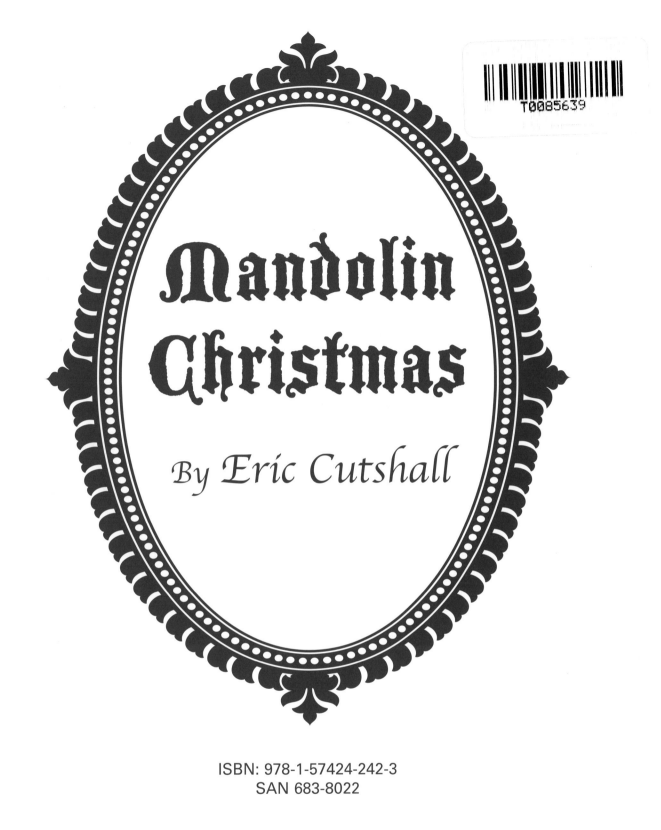

Mandolin Christmas

By Eric Cutshall

ISBN: 978-1-57424-242-3
SAN 683-8022

Cover photo: Morgan Monroe Mandolin courtesy of SHS International, www.shsint.net
Book and cover design by Eric Peterson

Copyright © 2008 CENTERSTREAM Publishing, LLC
P.O. Box 17878 - Anaheim Hills, CA 92817

www.centerstream-usa.com

Table of Contents

🌿 Foreword 🌿

Welcome to "Mandolin Christmas." There are three good reasons to learn to play Christmas songs:

1. They are familiar to most people.
2. Christmas songs sound good as solo arrangements.
3. You have 11 months to practice before you might have to perform them.

Each song is presented in two versions: a lead sheet and a solo arrangement. A lead sheet contains the melody, chords, and lyrics. You can play the melody on the mandolin or strum the chords while you sing the melody. This arrangement can also be fun to play with another mandolin player or guitar player. One person plays the melody while the other person strums the chords. The solo arrangement combines the melody and accompaniment which enhances the sound if you are playing by yourself. The solo arrangement will also sound good when played with another musician strumming chords. I suggest learning the single note melody in the lead sheet first before moving on to the solo arrangement. Some of the solo arrangements may be challenging to play at first as there are many quick chord changes and some new chord positions. If you find any passages difficult, practice them several times slowly and accurately. When you feel comfortable with them try playing them up to speed with the rest of the song. Each song is presented in standard music notation as well as Tablature.

If you are unfamiliar with some of the chords in this book I suggest you purchase "Mandolin Chords Plus" by Ron Middlebrook (00000040 – Centerstream Publishing). Not only does it feature over 300 chord fingerings, but also shows intros, endings, turnarounds, scales, how to read Tablature and even a couple of songs - all of that information for only $3.50. Be sure to check out some of the other books available from Centerstream. A small sample of their catalog is listed on the last page of this book.

Christmas only comes once a year but you can enjoy these songs all year long.

🌿 About the Author 🌿

Eric Cutshall grew up in a musical family. He developed an interest in music at an early age and began to play with a few of the instruments lying around the house including the guitar and banjo. His interests later expanded to mandolin, ukulele, and dulcimer. Eric received private music lessons throughout junior high and high school. After graduating, he continued his musical education at Musicians Institute in Hollywood, California. Eric has been a professional musician and music teacher for over twenty years. In addition to live performances throughout the United States and Europe, he has been featured on several recordings. For more information please visit his website: www.eric-cutshall.com.

Adeste Fideles (O Come All Ye Faithful)

Adeste Fideles (O Come All Ye Faithful)

Arr. Eric Cutshall

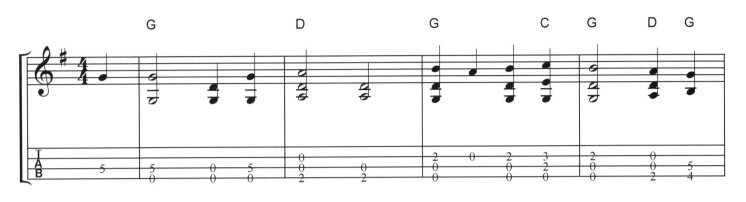

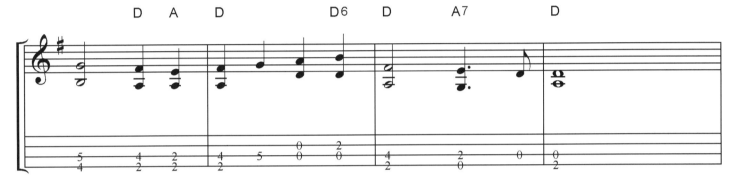

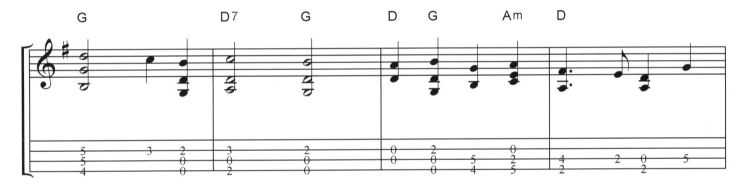

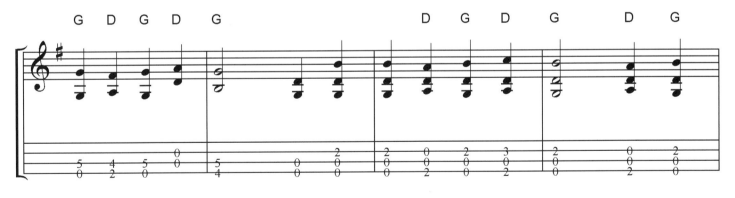

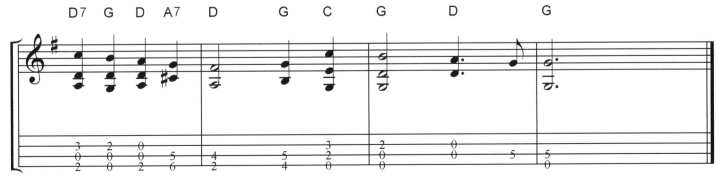

Angels We Have Heard On High

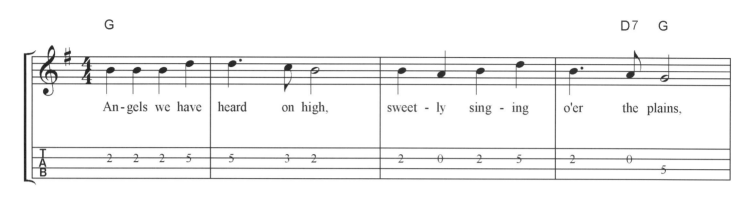

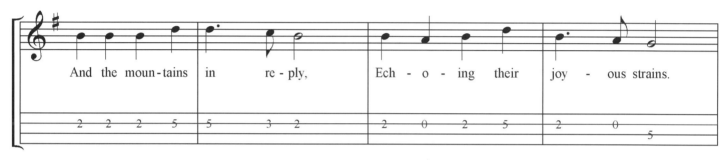

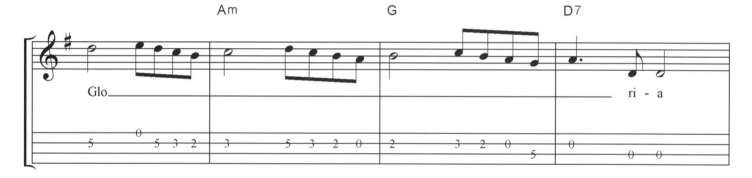

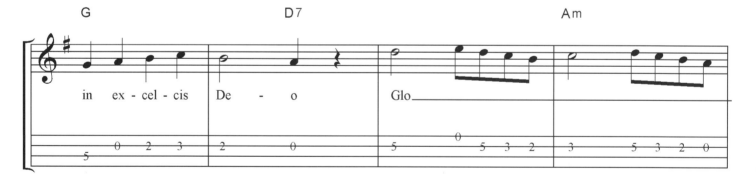

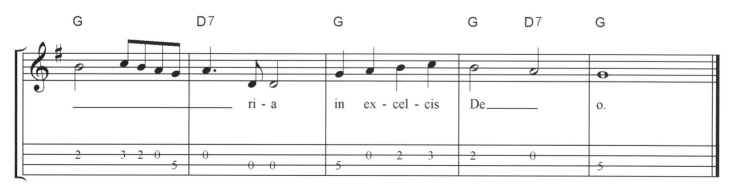

Angels We Have Heard On High

Arr. by Eric Cutshall

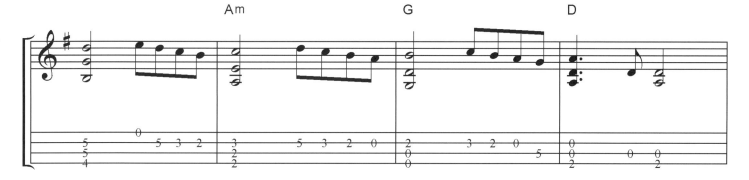

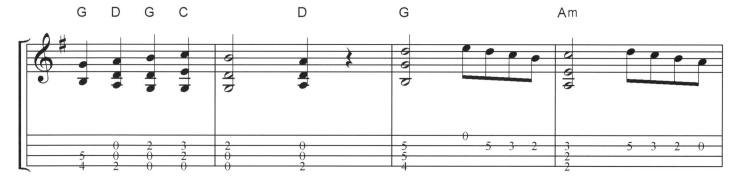

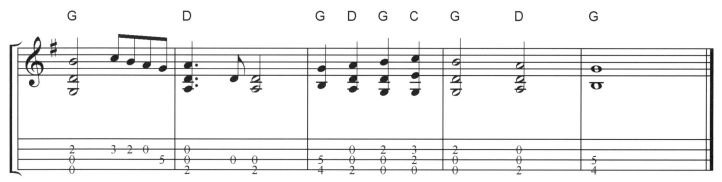

9

Away In A Manger

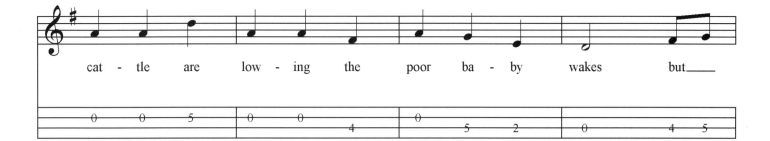

cat - tle   are   low - ing   the   poor   ba - by   wakes   but___

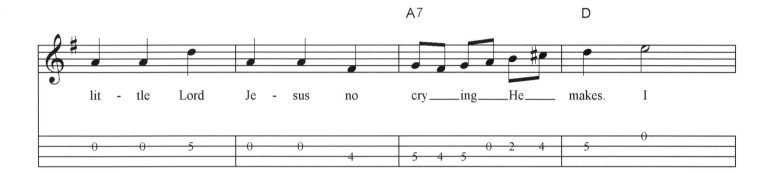

A7   D

lit - tle   Lord   Je - sus   no   cry___ing___He___   makes.   I

G   D7   G   C   G

love   Thee   Lord___   Je - sus   look   down   from   the   sky,   and

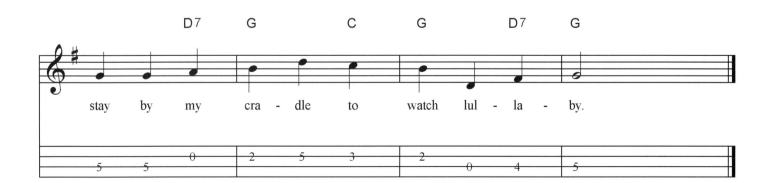

D7   G   C   G   D7   G

stay   by   my   cra - dle   to   watch   lul - la - by.

Away In A Manger

Arr. by Eric Cutshall

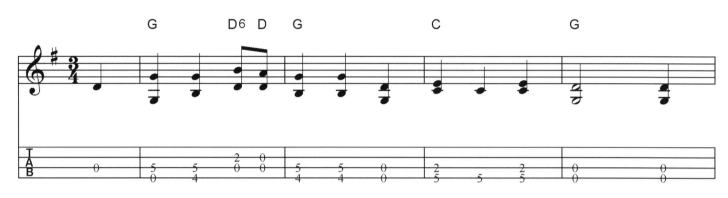

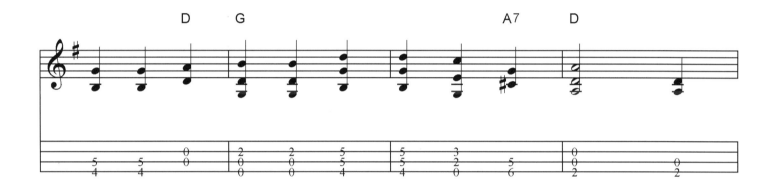

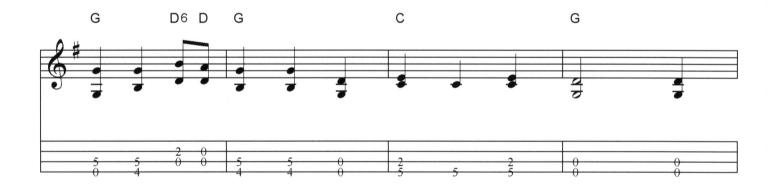

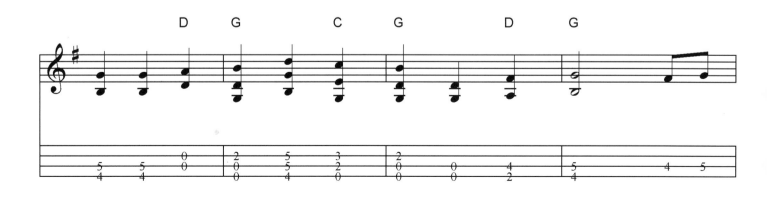

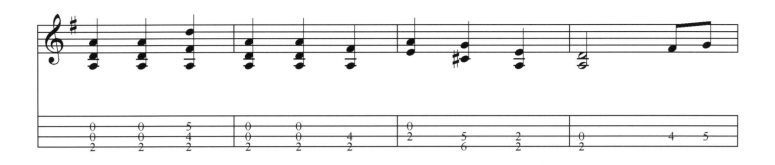

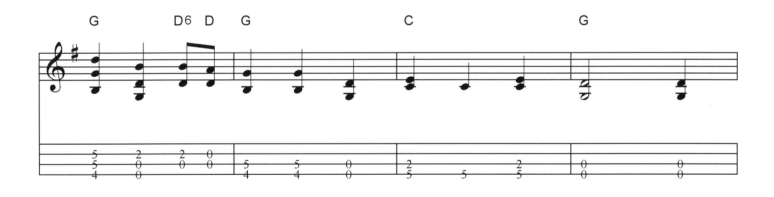

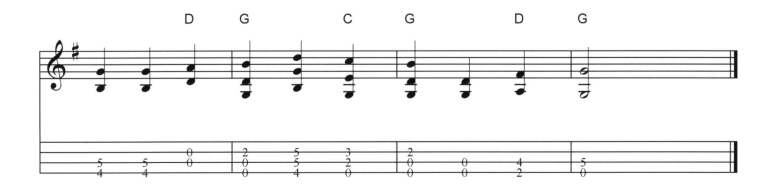

13

Deck The Halls

Deck The Halls

Arr. by Eric Cutshall

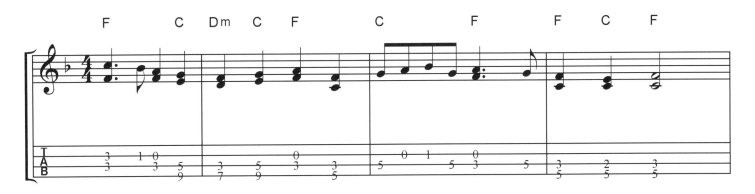

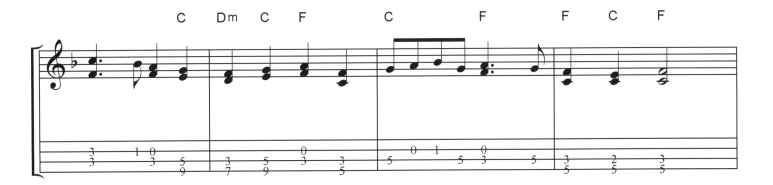

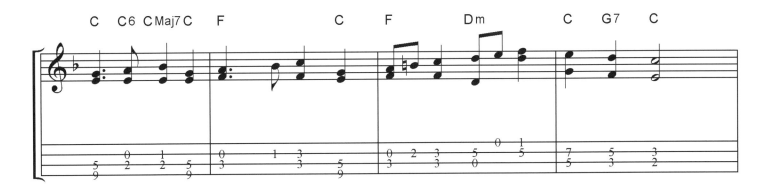

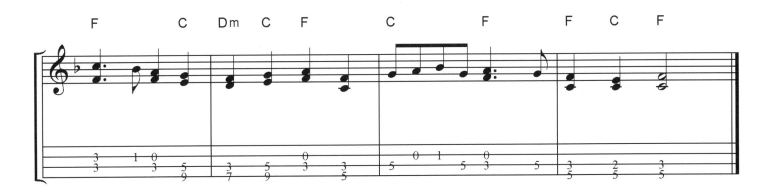

The First Noel

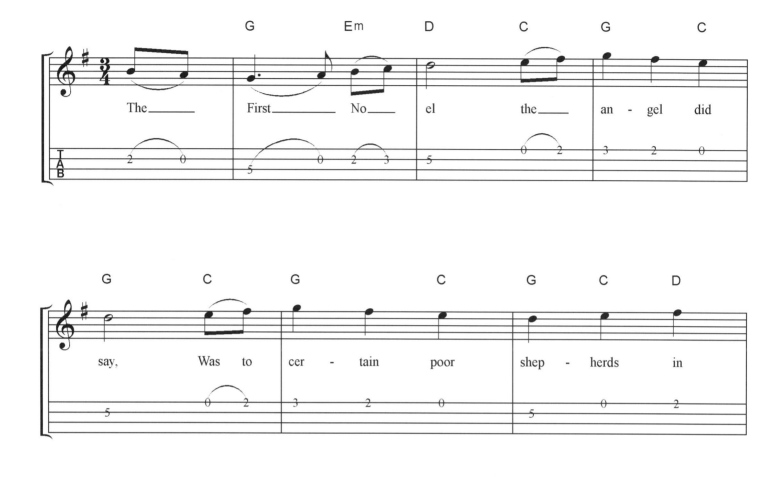

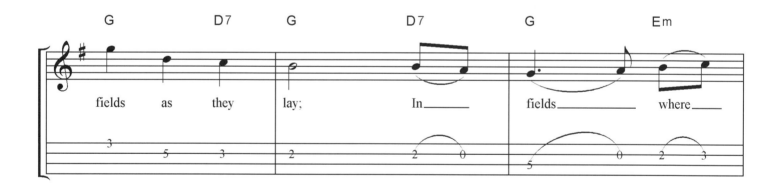

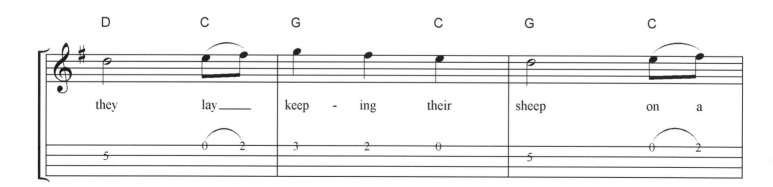

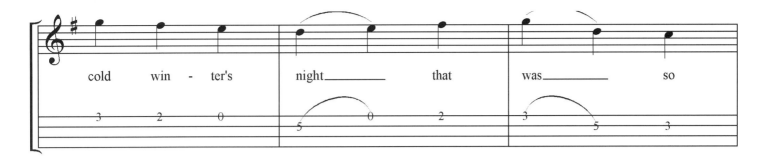

cold   win - ter's   night_____   that   was_____   so

deep.   No____   el_____   No____   el   No____

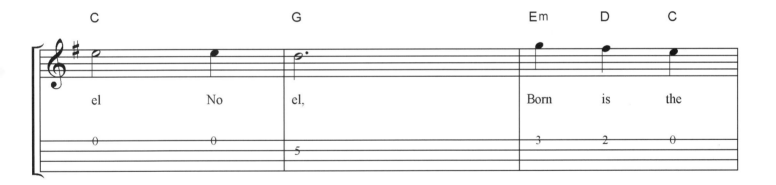

el   No   el,   Born   is   the

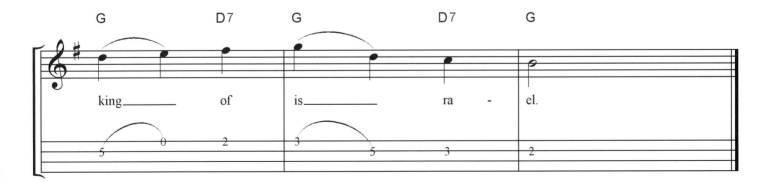

king_____   of   is_____   ra -   el.

The First Noel

Arr. by Eric Cutshall

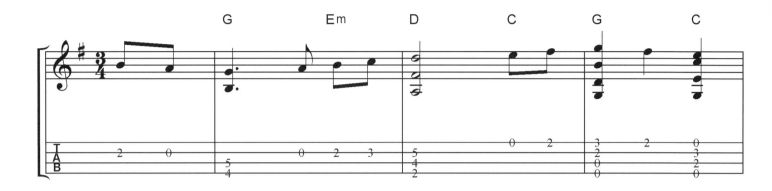

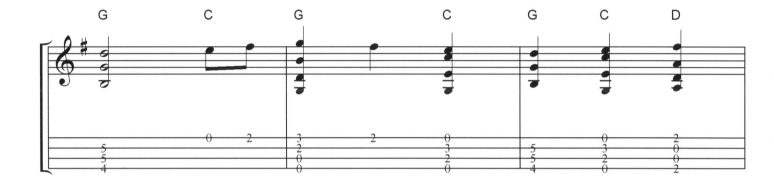

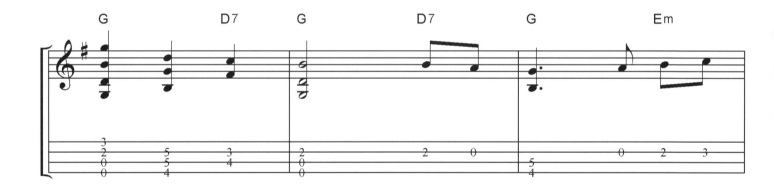

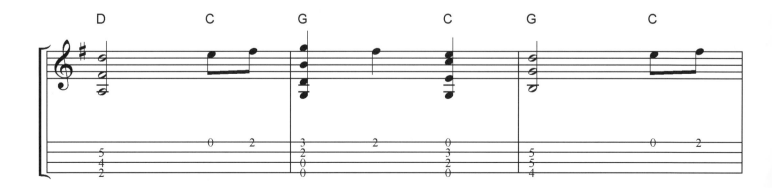

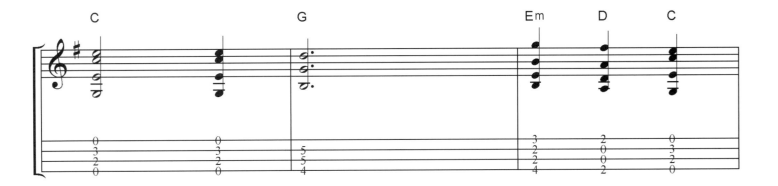

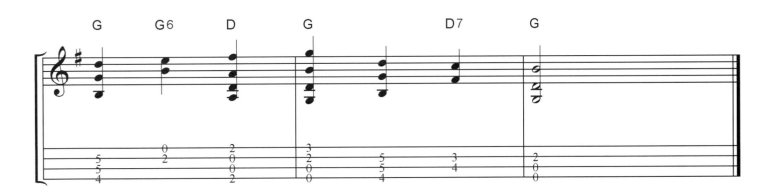

Go Tell It On The Mountain

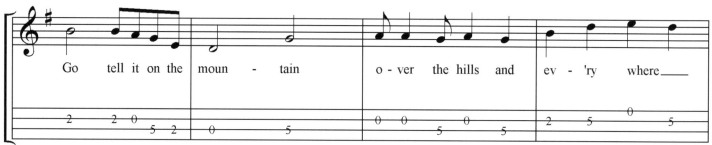

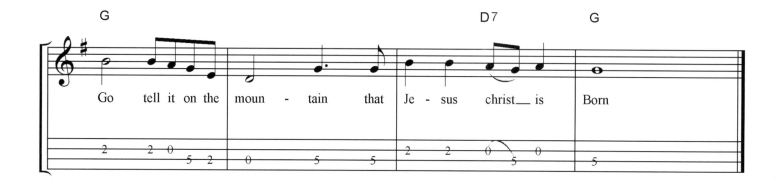

Go Tell It On The Mountain

Arr. by Eric Cutshall

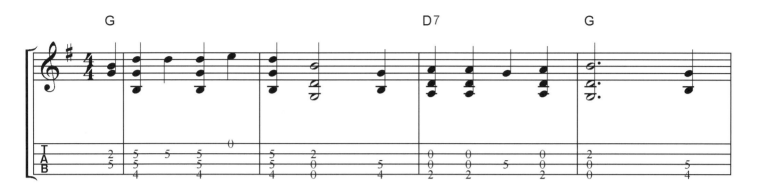

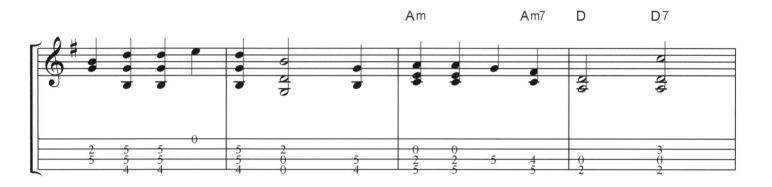

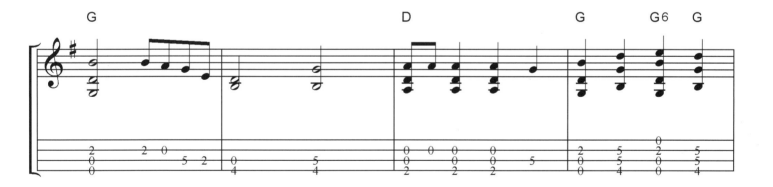

God Rest Ye Merry Gentlemen

God Rest Ye Merry Gentlemen

Arr. by Eric Cutshall

Good King Wenceslas

Good King Wenceslas

Arr. by Eric Cutshall

Hark! The Herald Angels Sing

Hark! The Herald Angels Sing

Arr. by Eric Cutshall

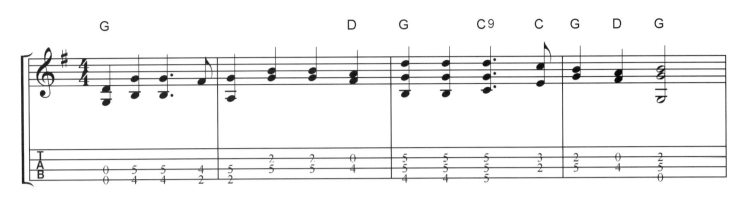

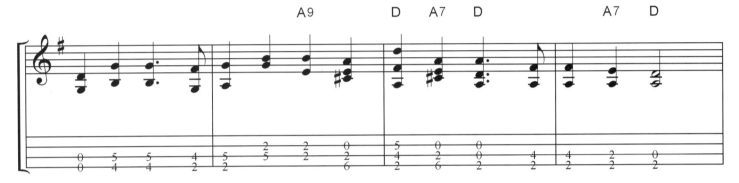

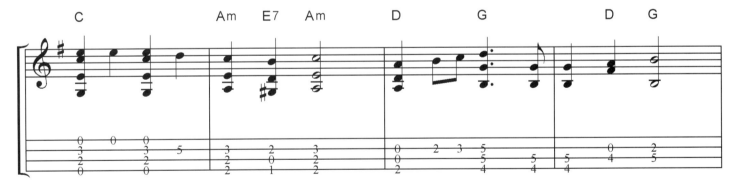

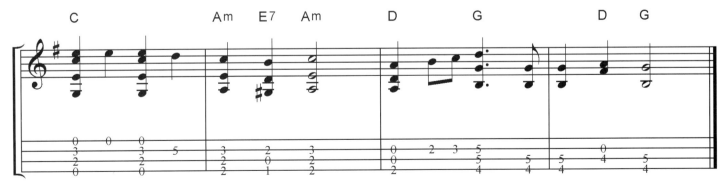

It Came Upon A Midnight Clear

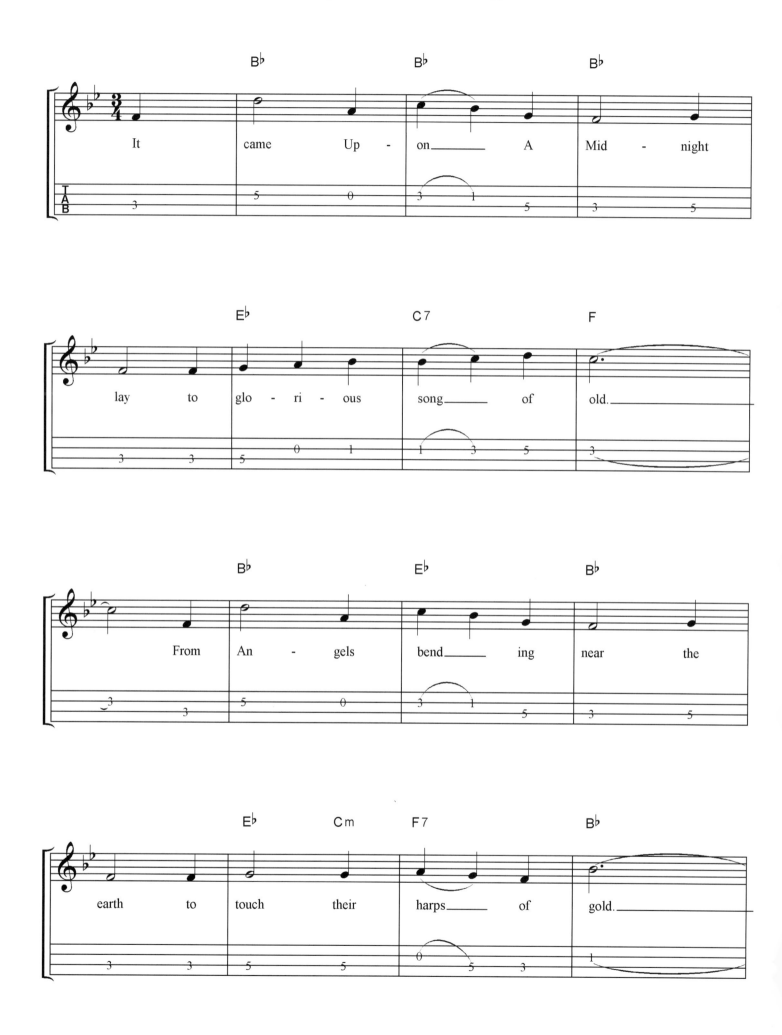

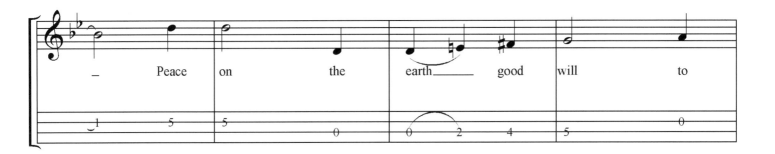

_ Peace on the earth_____ good will to

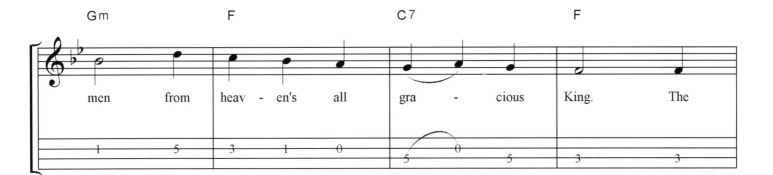

men from heav - en's all gra - cious King. The

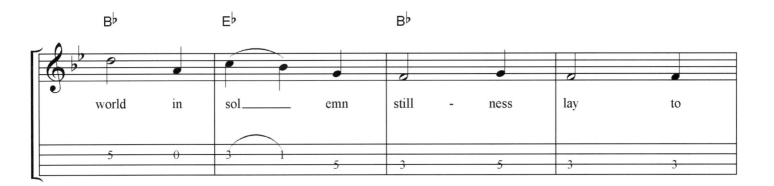

world in sol_____ emn still - ness lay to

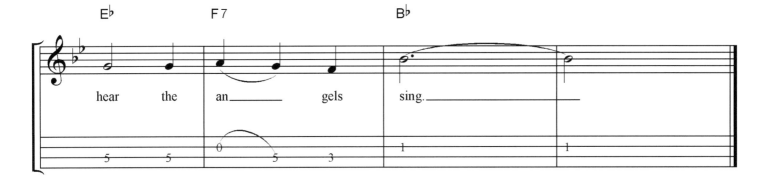

hear the an_____ gels sing._____

It Came Upon A Midnight Clear

Arr. by Eric Cutshall

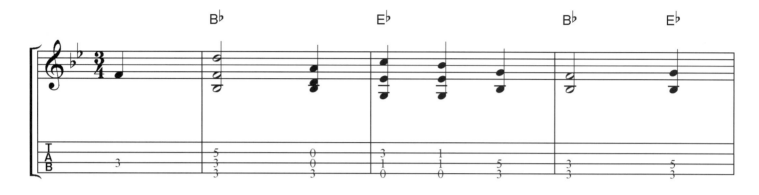

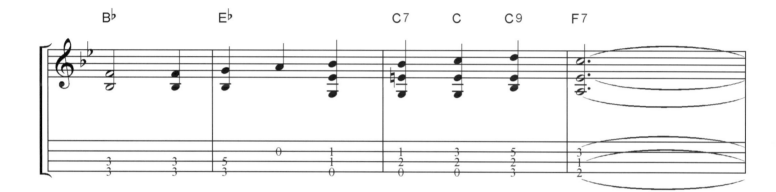

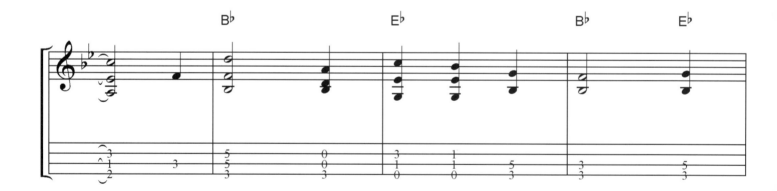

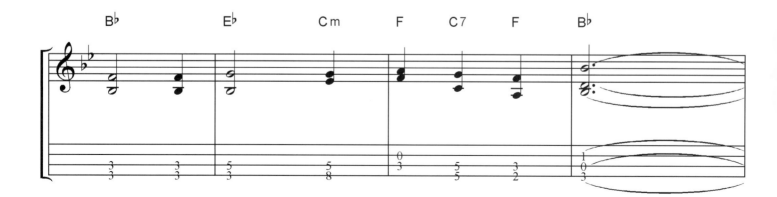

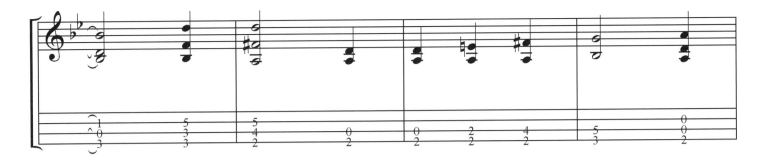

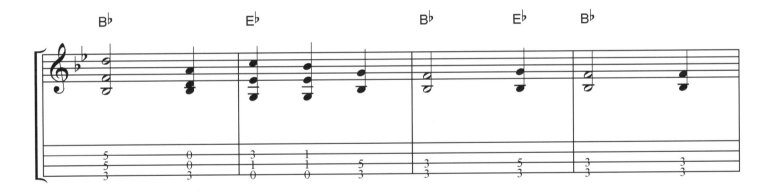

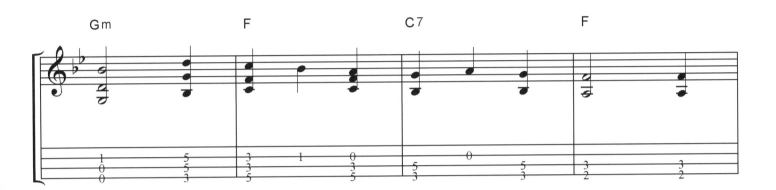

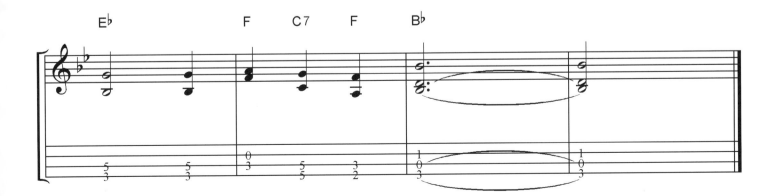

Jingle Bells

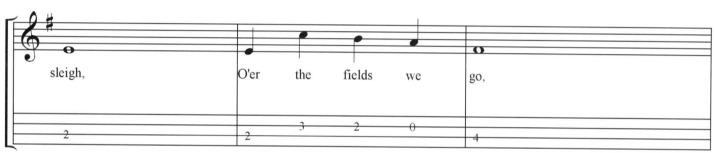

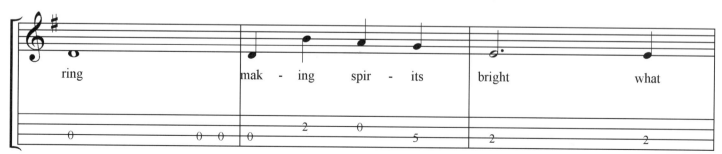

fun   it   is   to   ride   and   sing   a   sleigh - ing   song   to -

G

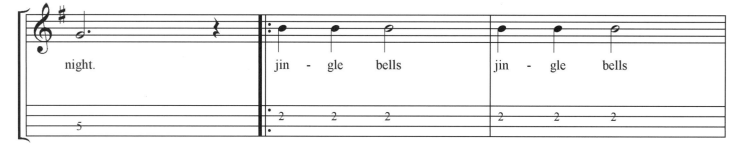

night.   jin - gle   bells   jin - gle   bells

C

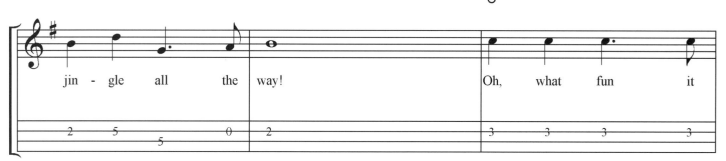

jin - gle   all   the   way!   Oh,   what   fun   it

G   **A7**   **D**   **D7**

is   to   ride   in   a   one   horse   o - pen   sleigh!   Oh,

D

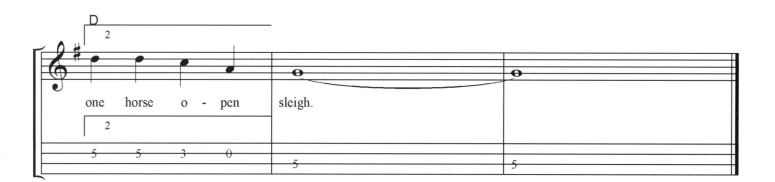

one   horse   o - pen   sleigh.

Jingle Bells

Arr. by Eric Cutshall

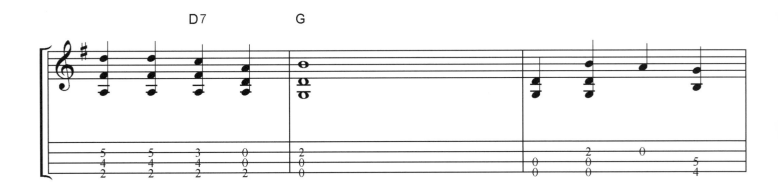

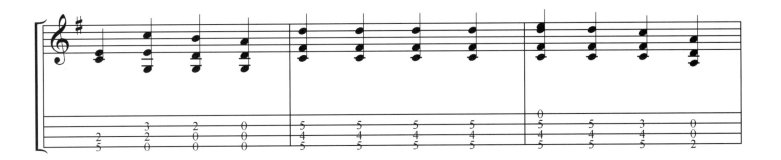

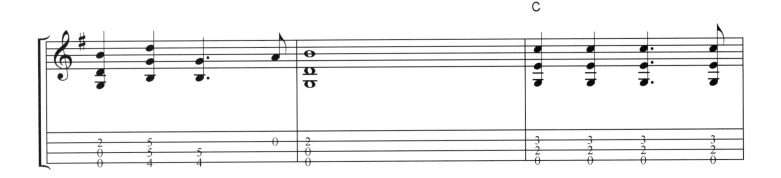

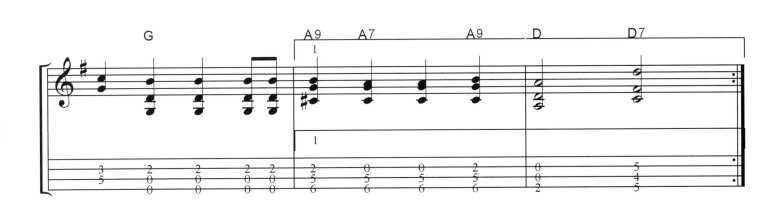

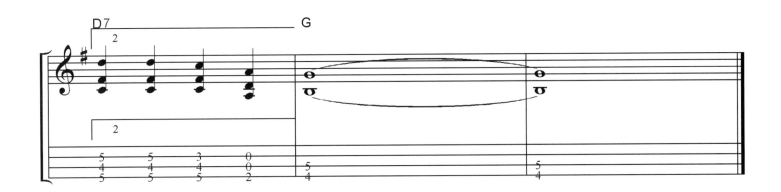

Jolly Old Saint Nicholas

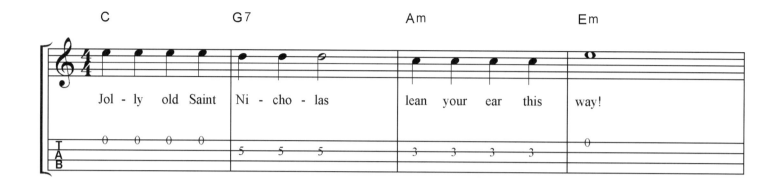

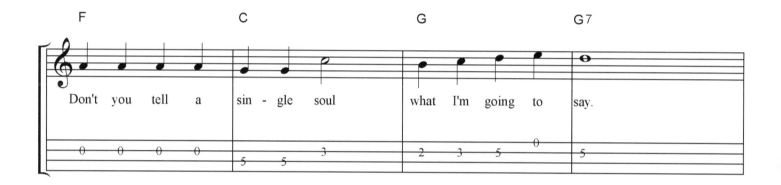

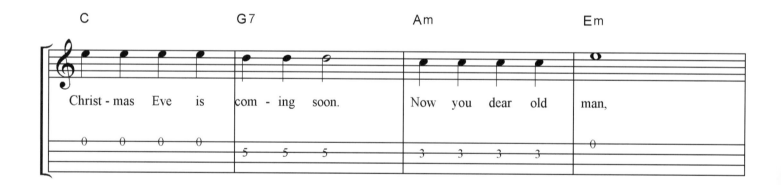

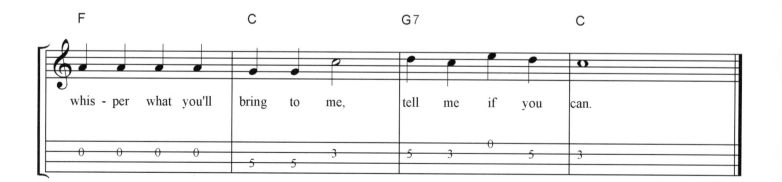

Jolly Old Saint Nicholas

Arr. by Eric Cutshall

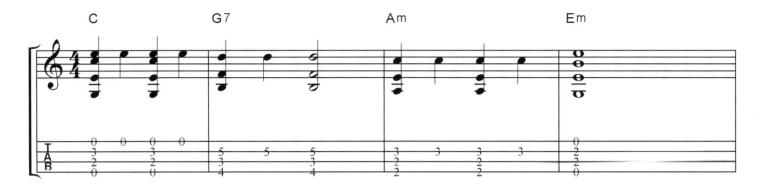

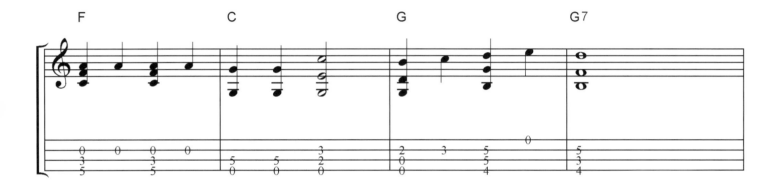

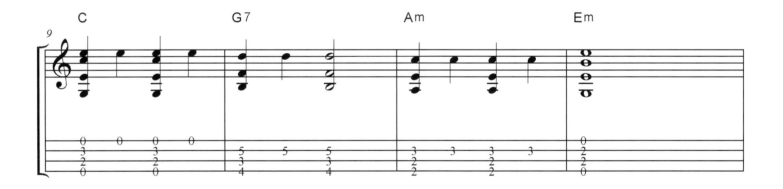

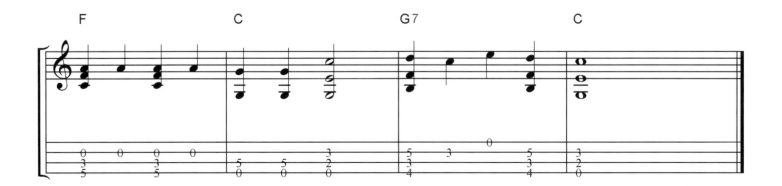

Joy To The World

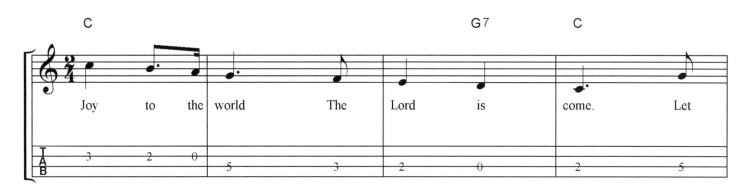

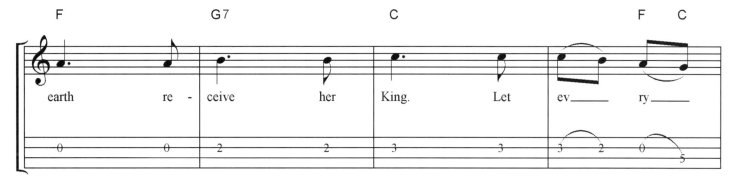

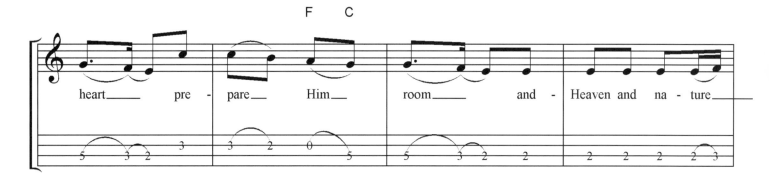

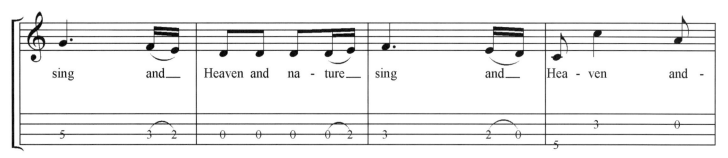

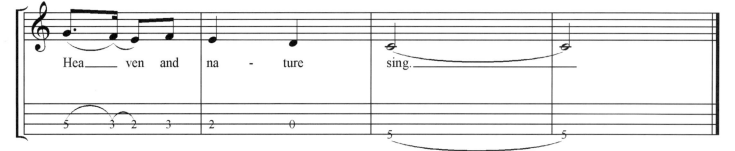

Joy To The World

Arr. by Eric Cutshall

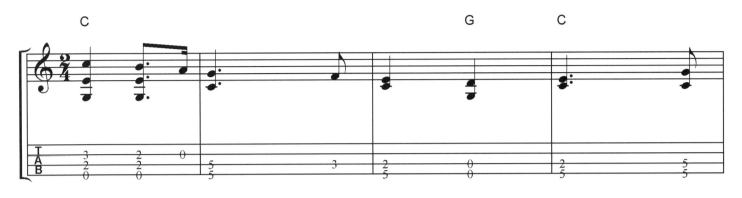

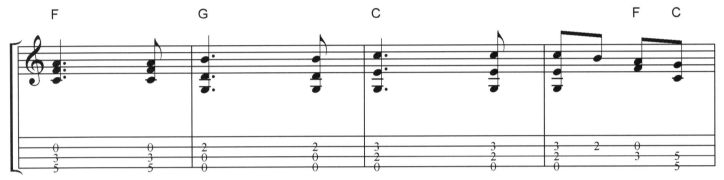

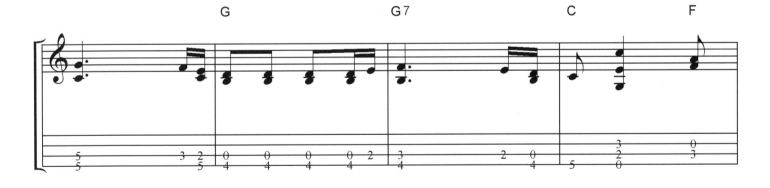

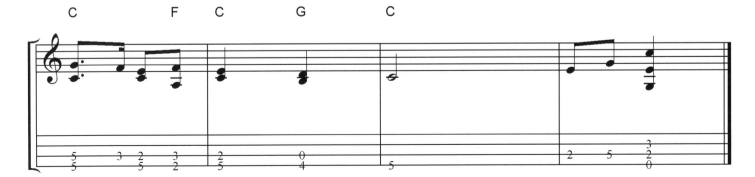

O Christmas Tree

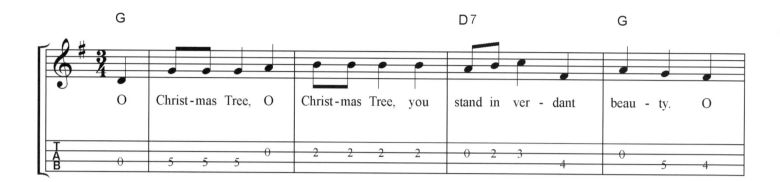

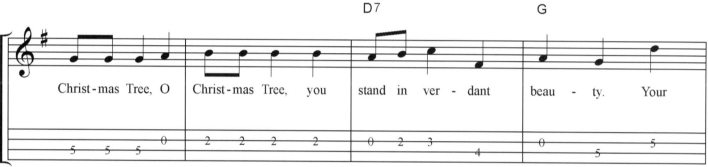

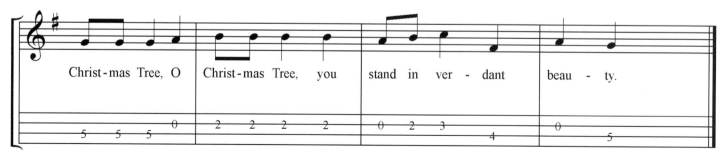

O Christmas Tree

Arr. by Eric Cutshall

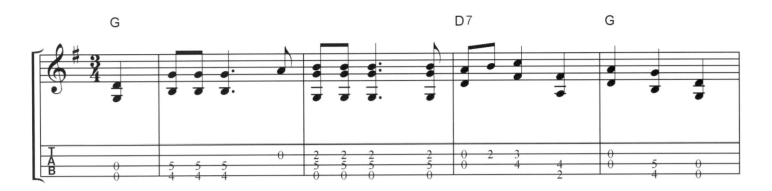

O Holy Night

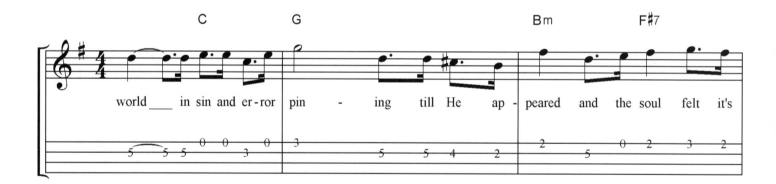

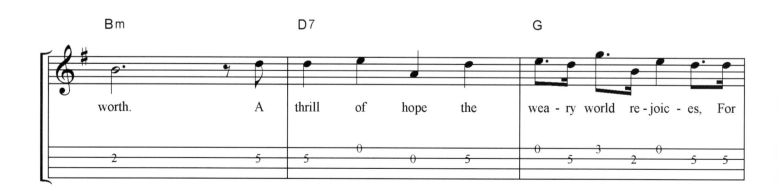

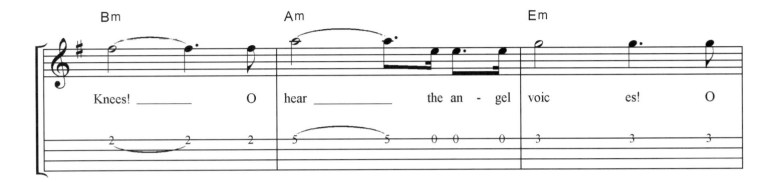

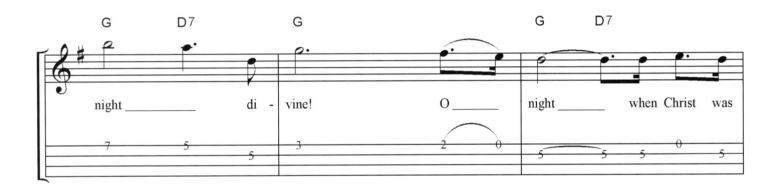

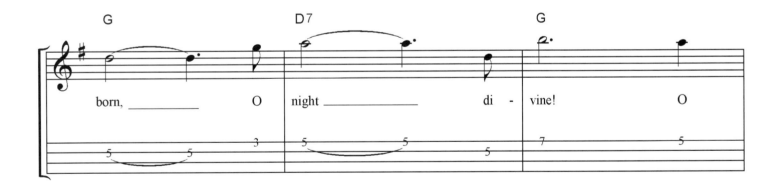

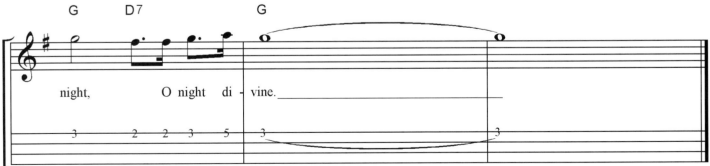

O Holy Night

Arr. by Eric Cutshall

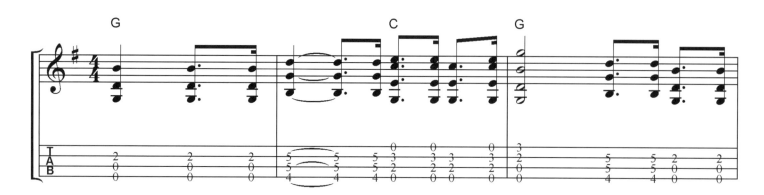

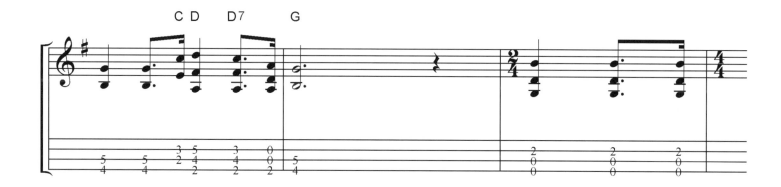

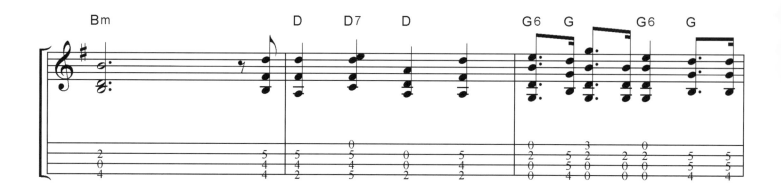

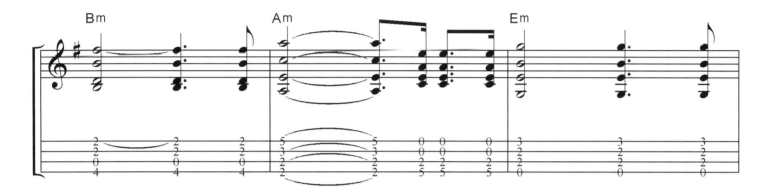

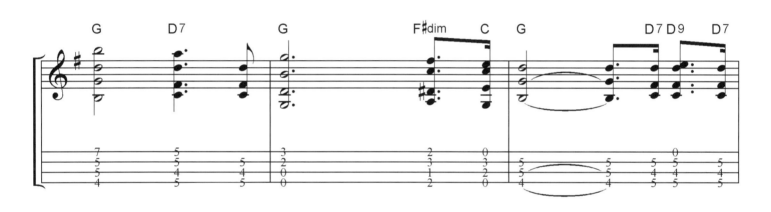

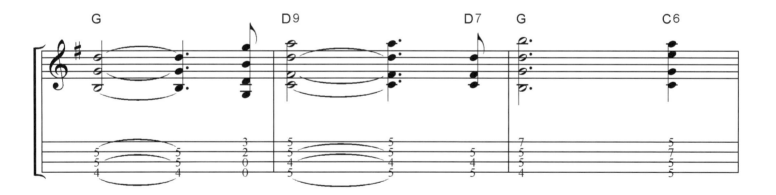

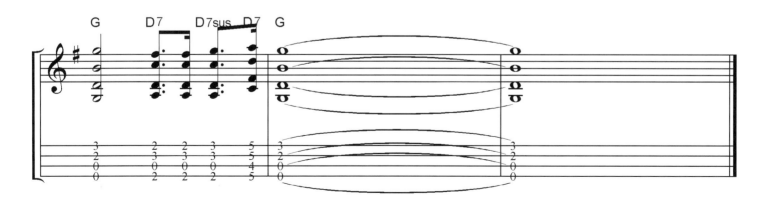

O Little Town Of Bethlehem

O Little Town Of Bethlehem

Arr. by Eric Cutshall

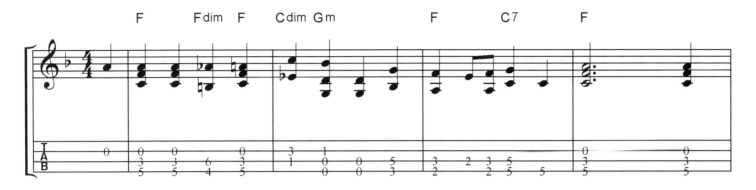

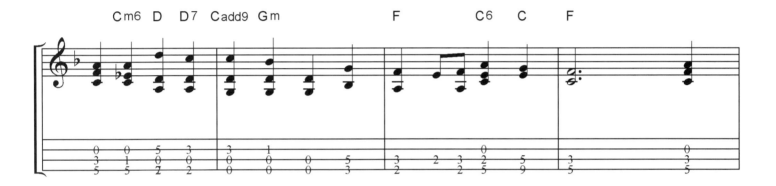

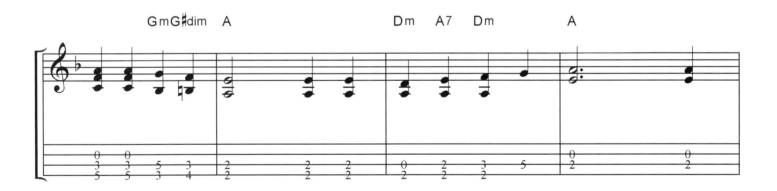

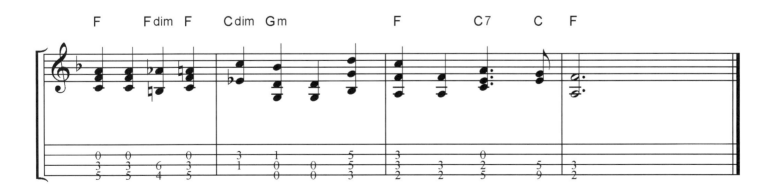

Silent Night

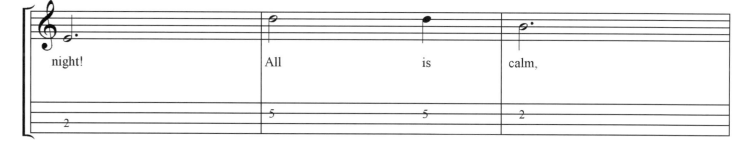

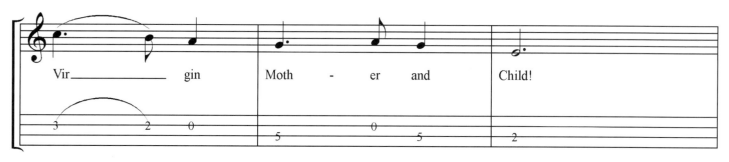

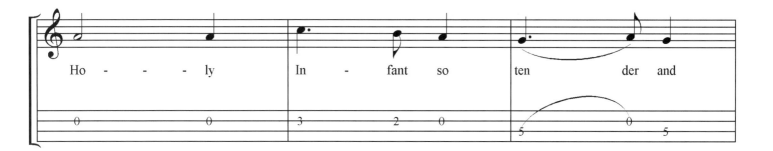

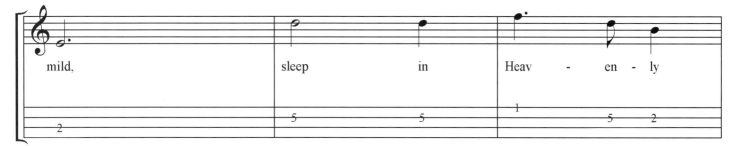

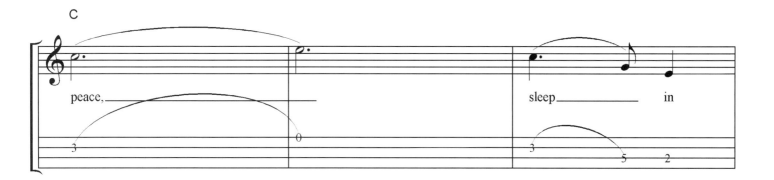

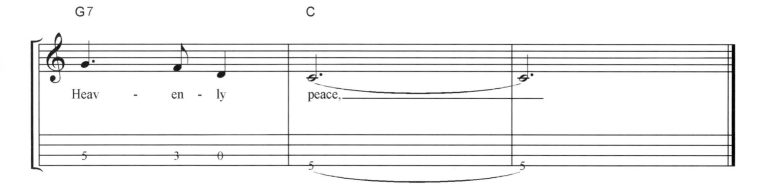

Silent Night

Arr. by Eric Cutshall

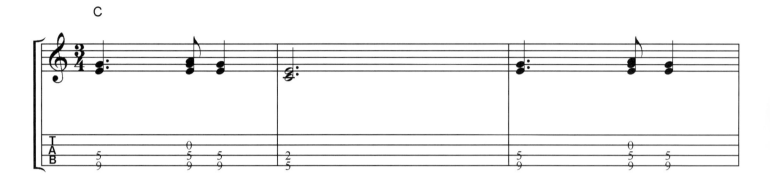

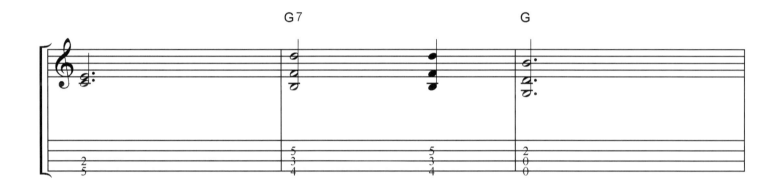

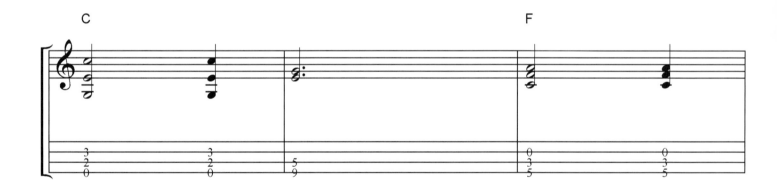

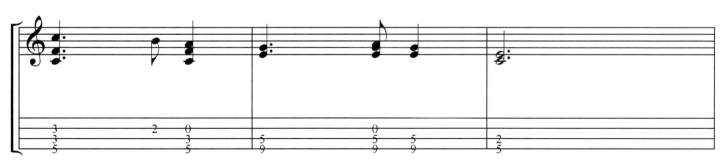

G7

C

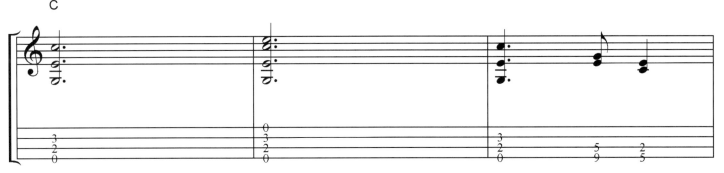

G7   C

We Three Kings Of Orient Are

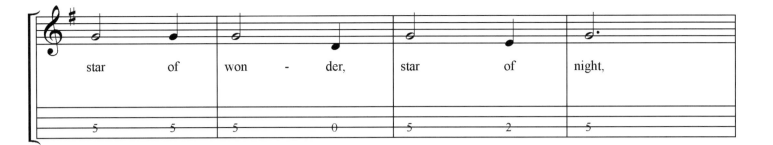

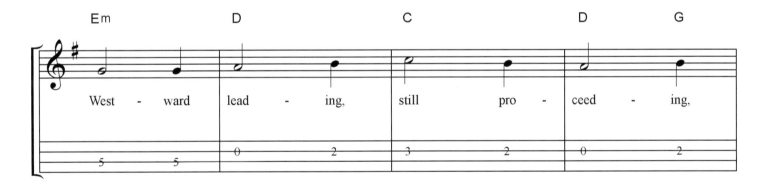

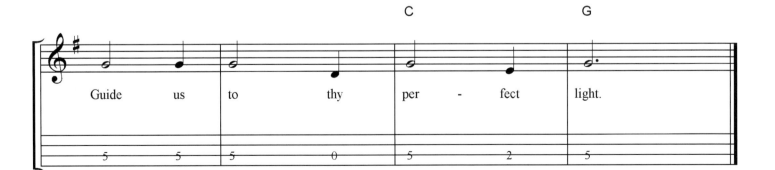

We Three Kings Of Orient Are

Arr. by Eric Cutshall

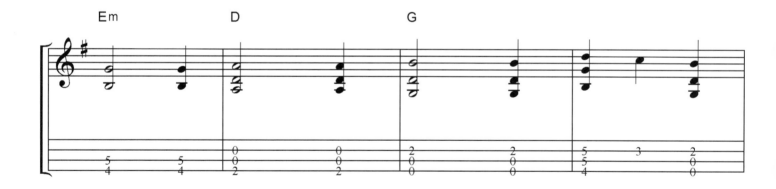

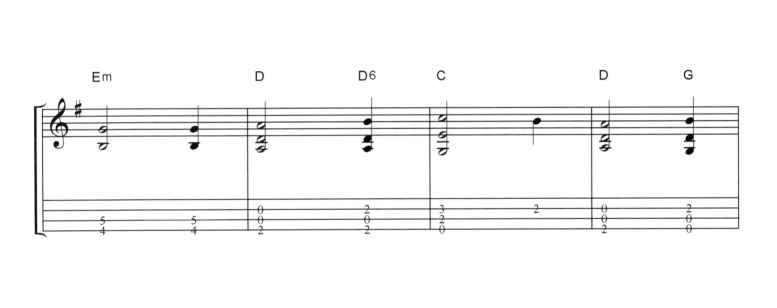

We Wish You A Merry Christmas

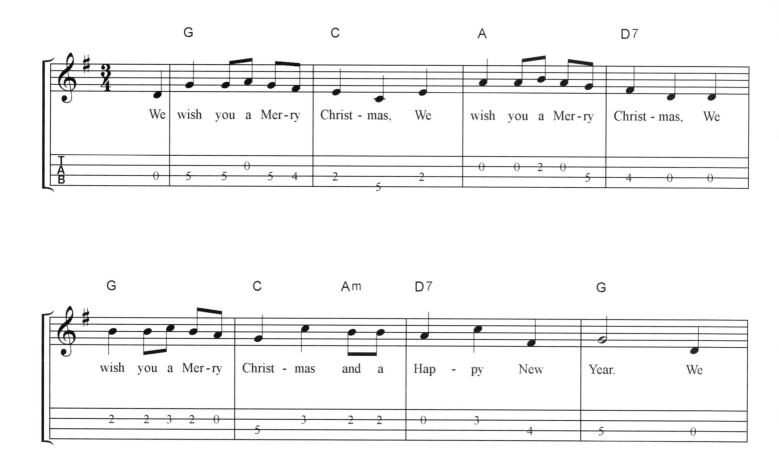

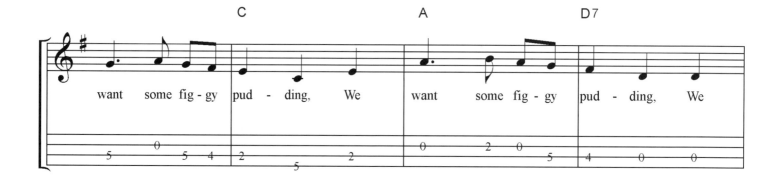

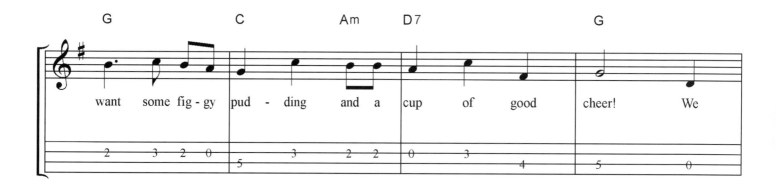

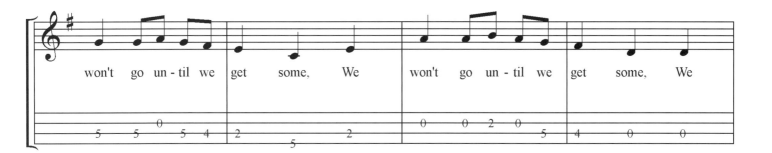

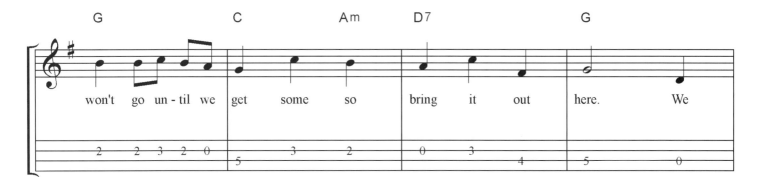

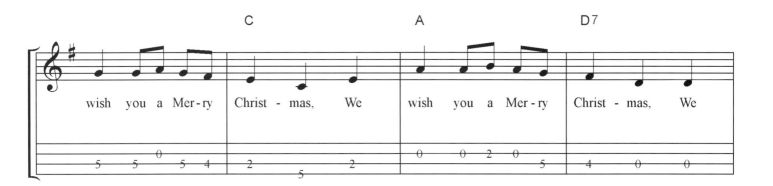

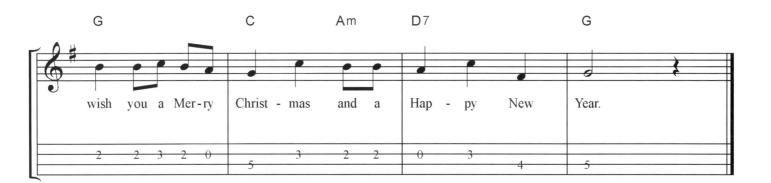

We Wish You A Merry Christmas

Arr. by Eric Cutshall

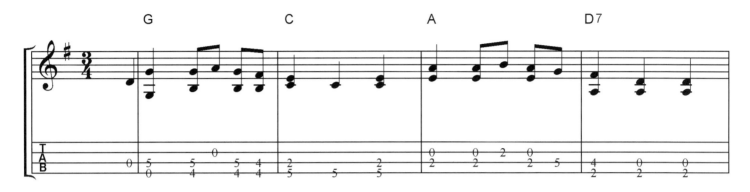

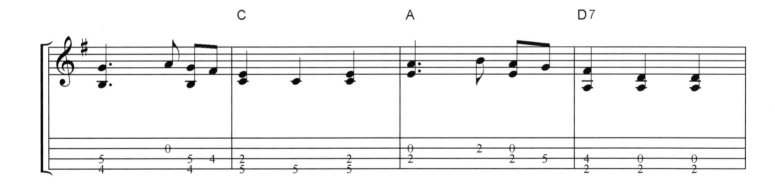

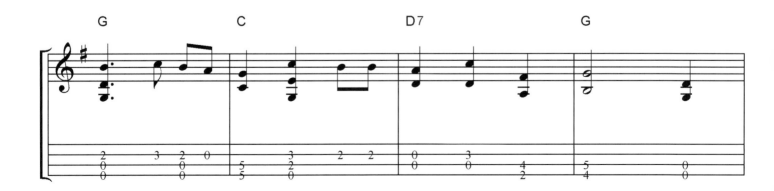

G   C   Am9   D7   G

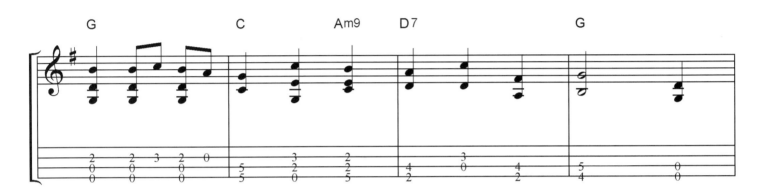

                           C   A   D7

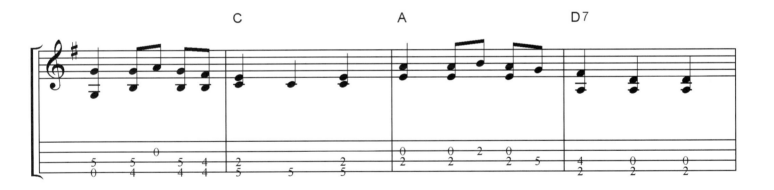

G   C   D7   G

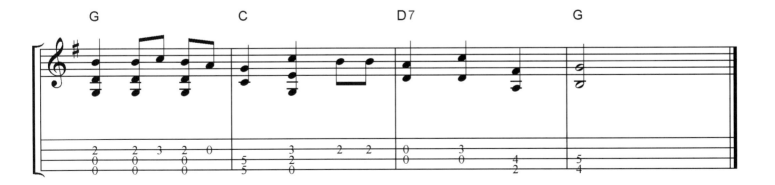

What Child Is This?

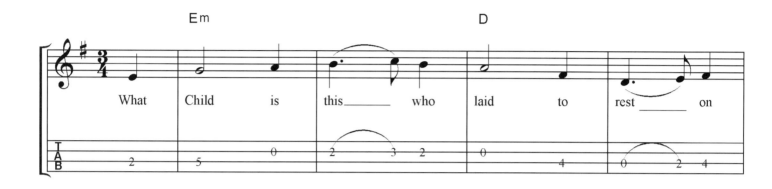

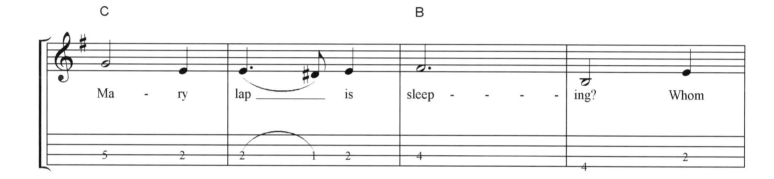

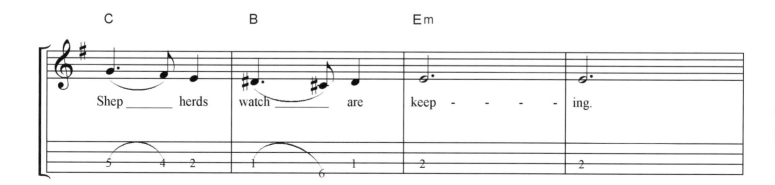

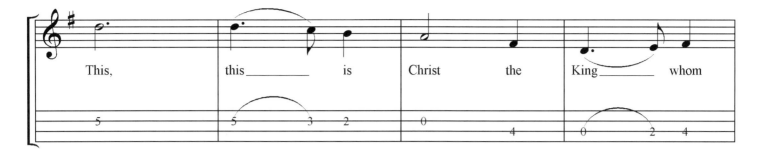

This, this_____ is Christ the King_____ whom

C   **B**

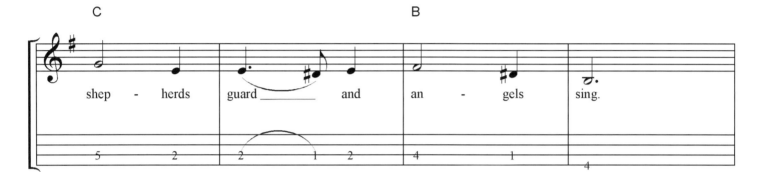

shep - herds guard_____ and an - gels sing.

G   **D**

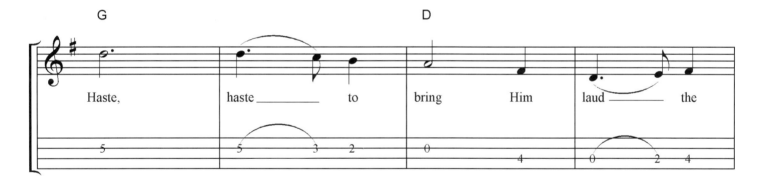

Haste, haste_____ to bring Him laud_____ the

C   **B**   **Em**

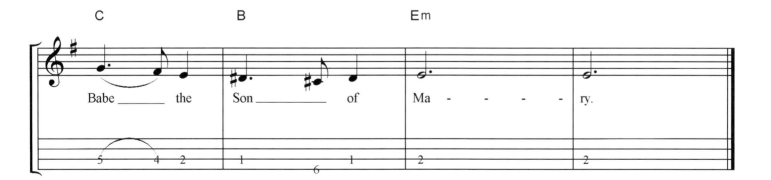

Babe _____ the Son _____ of Ma - - - ry.

What Child Is This?

Arr. by Eric Cutshall

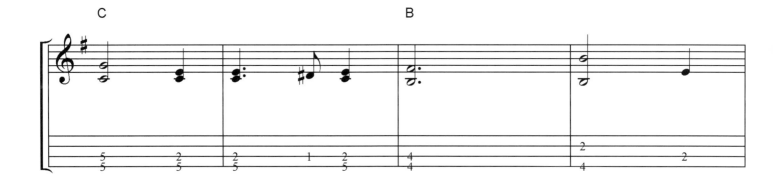

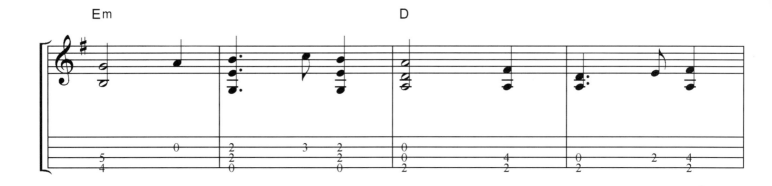

C · · · · · · · · · · B

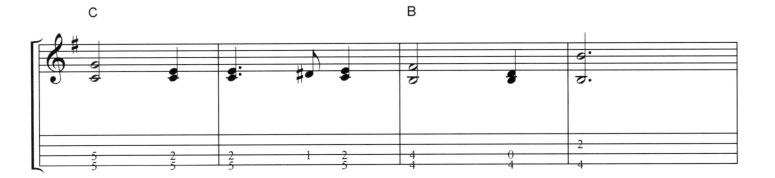

G · · · · · · · · · · D

C · · · · · B · · · · Em

More Great Christmas Books from Centerstream...

CHRISTMAS SOUTH OF THE BORDER
featuring the Red Hot Jalapeños
with special guest
The Cactus Brothers
Add heat to your holiday with these ten salsa-flavored arrangements of time-honored Christmas carols. With the accompanying CD, you can play your guitar along with The Cactus Brothers on: Jingle Bells • Deck the Halls • Silent Night • Joy to the World • What Child Is This? • and more. ¡Feliz Navidad!

00000319 Book/CD Pack $19.95

A CLASSICAL CHRISTMAS
by Ron Middlebrook
This book/CD pack features easy to advanced play-along arrangements of 23 top holiday tunes for classical/fingerstyle guitar. Includes: Birthday of a King • God Rest Ye, Merry Gentlemen • Good Christian Men, Rejoice • Jingle Bells • Joy to the World • O Holy Night • O Sanctissima • What Child Is This? (Greensleeves) • and more. The CD features a demo track for each song.

00000271 Book/CD Pack $15.95

CHRISTMAS UKULELE, HAWAIIAN STYLE
Play your favorite Christmas songs Hawaiian style with expert uke player Chika Nagata. This book/CD pack includes 12 songs, each played 3 times: the first and third time with the melody, the second time without the melody so you can play or sing along with the rhythm-only track. Songs include: Mele Kalikimaka (Merry Christmas to You) • We Wish You a Merry Christmas • Jingle Bells (with Hawaiian lyrics) • Angels We Have Heard on High • Away in a Manger • Deck the Halls • Hark! The Herald Angels Sing • Joy to the World • O Come, All Ye Faithful • Silent Night • Up on the Housetop • We Three Kings.

00000472 Book/CD Pack $19.95

JAZZ GUITAR CHRISTMAS
by George Ports
Features fun and challenging arrangements of 13 Christmas favorites. Each song is arranged in both easy and intermediate chord melody style. Songs include: All Through the Night • Angels from the Realm of Glory • Away in a Manger • The Boar's Head Carol • The Coventry Carol • Deck the Hall • Jolly Old St. Nicholas • and more.

00000240 .... $9.95

CHRISTMAS SOUTH OF THE BORDER
featuring The Cactus Brothers
with Special Guest
Señor Randall Ames
Add heat to your holiday with these Salsa-flavored piano arrangements of time-honored Christmas carols. Play along with the arrangements of Señor Randall Ames on Silent Night, Carol of the Bells, We Three Kings, Away in a Manger, O Come O Come Immanuel, and more. Feliz Navidad!

00000343 Book/CD Pack $19.95
00000345 Book/CD Pack $19.95

DOBRO CHRISTMAS
arranged by Stephen F. Toth
Well, it's Christmas time again, and you, your family and friends want to hear some of those favorite Christmas songs on your glistening (like the "trees") Dobro with its bell-like (as in "jingle") tone. This book contains, in tablature format, 2 versions of 20 classic Christmas songs plus a bonus "Auld Lang Syne" for your playing and listening pleasure. The arrangements were created to make them easy to learn, play, remember, or sight read. So get playing and get merry!

00000218 .... $9.95

CHRISTMAS MUSIC COMPANION FACT BOOK
by Dale V. Nobbman
For 50 beloved traditional tunes, readers will learn the story of how the song came to be, the author and the historical setting, then be able to play a great arrangement of the song! Songs examined include: Away in a Manger • Deck the Halls • Jingle Bells • Joy to the World • O Christmas Tree • O Holy Night • Silver Bells • We Wish You a Merry Christmas • What Child Is This? • and more!

00000272 112 pages $12.95

THE ULTIMATE CHRISTMAS MUSIC COMPANION FACT BOOK
by Dale Nobbman
This book provides comprehensive biographical sketches of the men and women who wrote, composed, and translated the most famous traditional Christmas songs of all time. Their true-life stories and achievements are fascinating and inspirational for anyone wanting to know more about the people behind the music. 144 pages.

00001178 .... $24.95

P.O. Box 17878 - Anaheim Hills, CA 92817
(714) 779-9390   www.centerstream-usa.com